The Maze

The Maze

A daydream in five cantos

DAVID MORPHET

First published in 2009 by

Notion Books
11 Daisy Lane
London
SW6 3DD
www.notionbooks.co.uk

ISBN 09541573 6 2

Canto One

Late in the year, one morning I awoke
and found myself shut in on every side
by high and thorny hedges, with a cloak

of thick fog everywhere. There was no hide
or hut; no sound, no voice; nothing to show
location or bearing; nothing to guide –

only a narrow alley where, with slow
steps, I moved between the hedges, feeling
my way, the mist swirling, my courage low.

As day wore on, the haze dispersed, revealing
long lines of foliage with intersections
and dead ends. I knew then I was dealing

with a maze, full of obscure deflections,
with walls which blocked me off or led me on,
sending me back and forth in all directions.

Each broad way would turn out to be a sham;
and all the work of threading twist and turn
be lost as I came back where I began.

Deception followed deception. No return
seemed possible; no exit from these pounds
of lost content; no end you could discern.

The alleys seemed to have elastic bounds:
the more I walked, the further they would go;
the junctions multiplied, the high surrounds

grew higher, darker, and the sun dropped low.
Then to my horror, at an alley's end,
I saw a black dog prowling to and fro.

If it attacked, I'd no way to defend
myself. I looked for somewhere I could hide.
I'd seen a little pathway round a bend,

and scuttled back; hoped for a hole to slide
out of the reach of slavering canine jaws.
Amazed, I saw a door, and slipped inside

as the animal approached. Without a pause
I slammed the bolt; made sure my barricade.
Outside, I heard the rattle-scratch of claws.

Turning around, I saw a gentle glade,
and then a garden full of shrubs and flowers,
with curving paths, and lawns, and temples made

of shells, and statues set in marbled bowers;
a frame for pineapples; a hanging vine;
a folly topped with ornamental towers;

a grotto lined with pebbles, like a shrine –
after the maze, an Eden of a place.
'Good Day, Sir,' said a high voice, 'I opine

your visit was unplanned, so pale your face,
so torn your garments.' Looking down, I found
a tiny man, his back held in a brace,

his shape contorted, and his forehead crowned
with a kind of cloche I'd somehow seen before.
'You're free by all means, Sir, to look around,'

the apparition said. 'Please do explore
the curiosities (here two "ahems").
It's here that I have laboured to restore

the glories of my garden by the Thames
at Twickenham, which once enjoyed some fame,
together with my rhymes and apothegms.'

I said, 'You do not need to tell your name;
you are the poet Alexander Pope
who wrote *The Rape*'. He bowed his head – 'The same:

the master of the well-turned line and trope
is he who owns this orderly retreat
and civil habitat.' 'And may one hope,'

I asked, 'to find an exit from your seat
which does not lead one back towards the hound
(or hounds) from which I've just made my retreat?'

'The maze,' he answered, 'stretches all around.
From my domain there is a single gate
into the web from which you've just unwound.

It is my whole endeavour to create
an ordered refuge, from the maze aside;
to live in comfort on my own estate,

and cultivate my garden, undenied.
All that I want lies here within this wall.
The dogs of ignorance run wild outside.

The feast of reason and the flow of soul
with chosen friends is all that I desire.'
This wasn't what I'd hoped to hear at all.

The drawbridge rhapsody did not inspire;
what I was after was a quick way out
with cover guaranteed, not friendly fire

from poets hunkered down in a redoubt
surrounded by their labyrinthine fears.
I thought it well to show some signs of doubt.

'But don't you wish to live among your peers?'
I asked. 'The life you lead seems so confined –
isn't reclusion bound to lead to tears?

Are other men of genius resigned
to horticulture? Nectarine and peach
may not be meat enough for every mind?'

'I cannot speak,' he said, 'for others. Each
much manage as he can: this does for me.
Ornament and abri are what I preach,

but some may like things simpler: the degree
is down to taste. The principle remains –
our choice is circumscribed: we are not free.

Our destiny's enclosure – all that restrains
encroachment and invasion and decay.
Whether it's clearings, gardens, grand domains,

however unadorned, however gay,
they each must build their wattle or their wall
to hold their own and keep the maze at bay.'

I found the poet's tale began to pall,
but how could I escape his gilded cage?
It did not take much effort to recall

the black dog which was lurking just off-stage,
and other alleys might have equal terrors,
or even worse – I had no way to gauge.

But in the trust that winners must be darers,
I asked the poet for his frank advice.
'Good Sir,' I said, 'I put it to you, whereas

I'm terrified to risk the wild maze twice,
I don't believe that I can trouble you
for more than say, a night, to be precise.

Is there some person who could steer me through
the passageways towards a further goal,
ensuring that I don't go all askew?'

His face showed much relief. 'Upon my soul,'
he said, 'my gardener John will be your guide;
he knows the safest alleys to patrol.

The time to travel's when the shadows slide
under the hedges for their mid-day rest;
and all the prowling dogs sleep stupefied:

siesta is the time that you'll find best.'
So John and I at twelve o'clock next day,
armed with stout sticks, and ready for the test,

slipped through the gate and set off on our way.

Canto Two

Said John, as we passed by a sleeping hound,
'I'm glad of the excuse to get away:
there's more to life than dibbling in the ground

and weeding round the quincunx every day.
The little gentleman back there can wait
until we've got you safely on your way.

I know the alleys and can educate
you in their inwardness, and take you where
you'll find a path ahead, however late.'

Astonished by this statement, and his care,
which made me wonder if I'd heard him right,
I asked him why the servant didn't share

his master's love of walls, and appetite
for living life within an ivory tower.
Surely he ought to be a satellite

around Pope's sun? And how to overpower
the maze's dangers? And how could he know
whether I'd find his lessons sweet or sour?

'Some people stay within,' he said. 'I go
to find the tools I cannot make alone;
and barter what I need for what I grow.

The maze is a bazaar where I can hone
my skills, bring them to market – not a threat.
The flag of self-sufficiency is flown

by those who never step outside, and yet
are glad to take the benefits of trade,
preferring as they take them to forget

the ones who feel the heat and smell the blade,
who take the risks, and know they must engage,
who aren't afraid to call a spade a spade.

And so I leave my master's gilded cage
and move about. The dangers are mere spaniels –
hounds which an ounce of offal will assuage.

There's nothing like a lion's den for Daniels
where we are going, though the Doctor's bark
is sharp enough, and you must be quite canny, else

he'll put you down: his humour's brusque and dark.
Let's press on. When the time's ripe I'll reveal
the meaning of my throwaway remark

about your path ahead, and how you'll feel.
Just follow where I lead, and you will find
our journey is a search, not an ordeal.'

A pause for thought – I didn't feel inclined
to ask his view just now on other small
conundrums which were running through my mind

like how I'd got into the maze at all,
or how we'd fare when every way was barred.
I simply asked on whom we were to call,

and why he'd warned me to be on my guard.
'Our neighbour, Dr Johnson,' he replied,
'is not a man for folly or façade,

and he's unhappy anywhere outside
his study where he's working to revise
some book with which he's never satisfied.

He won't walk in the maze, which he decries
as bleak and lacking in society.
The Doctor's never slow to criticise –

the faintest hint of impropriety
and down he thunders like a ton of bricks.
Irascible, a man of piety,

unkempt, encyclopaedic, he's a mix
of moralist and bully, so watch out.
Keep off religion. Same with politics.'

I said, 'The record here on walkabout
is unimpressive. Yet another chap
who likes to stay at home. I start to doubt

if Dr Johnson will have any map
to show the twists and turnings through the maze,
or teach us how to dodge a booby trap

if all he does is suck his pen and gaze
at words. There's no salvation to be found
in definitions, or a well-turned phrase.

But don't you worry. I won't go aground:
I'll trim my sails to what he has to say,
however academic or unsound.'

Said John, 'You'll get much more than a display
of erudition. He's a wise old Bard.
Cheer up. Let's not arrive in disarray.'

We turned into a narrow cobbled yard,
a Georgian town-house half-glimpsed at the end
through dusty foliage. We hammered hard

and listened till we heard loud steps descend
from upper floors. The door was opened wide.
There Johnson stood in all his bulk. 'Dear friend,'

he said to my companion, 'come inside.
And you, Sir, too are welcome to my lair.
I fear you'll find us very countrified.'

We followed as he shambled up the stair
into the study where his great work lay
cut up and scattered, bits on every chair.

'The next edition's due out any day,'
he muttered darkly, 'when this harmless drudge
can find out what is meant by *motorway*.'

I let this go, despite a gentle nudge
from John. *A road from Hell: a future curse*
would never do for an Augustan judge.

I seized the earliest moment to rehearse
my wish to quit the maze and all its works.
'You're rather late in life,' he said, 'to nurse

hopes of that colour, but all men have quirks.
I wrote the *History of Rasselas*
to edify the people whom it irks

to be confined by circumstance. Alas!
there's none that make a perfect choice of life:
a pleasing prospect oft ends in morass.

In all our study, fallacies are rife,
and when at last the message gets across,
the pain of learning cuts men like a knife,

and leaves them ill-equipped to fix a course
with any feeling it will meet success.
Indeed, for fear of finding something worse,

many decide it's better to unstress,
and let life's current take them where it will –
instead of acquisition, acquiesce.

Ambition fades – all fail with age – but still
men must endure, as Edgar said in *Lear*.
Passivity must be our codicil.

Bear this in mind when you depart from here
and travel through the maze to seek escape:
the world is Delphic: things are never clear.'

My view of Johnson took a sombre shape
after this homily. 'He's worse than Pope,'
I thought, 'a real Job's comforter in crepe.'

Nothing he said had given any hope
of new directions, nothing to inspire,
or satisfy, or show one how to cope.

I said to my companion, 'This is dire.
We're getting nowhere – let us say farewell,
and leave the Grand Cham sitting by his fire.'

So on we travelled, as the evening fell.

Canto Three

From time to time, John gave a sidelong glance
to judge my mood, waiting a while to see
me simmer down, swallow my petulance.

No bed; no supper, was the penalty
for jumping up and hurrying away,
with no word of regret, discourteously.

The right reaction would have been to stay
and Boswell out the meaning of his sombre
admonition – not make a vain display

of irritation. (Yes, and still the ember
burned within me: the insinuation
that escape was hopeless – better to surrender

to the flow; forget about liberation!)
At last John said, 'You made a mess of that;
and can't afford to in your situation.

The Doctor is a touchy autocrat,
but don't ignore his maxims and advice
because they may sound pompous or too pat.

He's right – the maze deceives, is imprecise.
You can't expect to find the things you hope,
and if a chance comes once, it won't come twice.

But don't despair. I'll be the mountain rope
that holds you steady as you look for holds;
the helping hand to pull you up the slope.'

The evening alleys shimmered now in folds
of silver, as the full moon poured down light
from its high spout, into the hedges' moulds.

So lit, we pressed on, always gaining height,
until, at the hill's crest, we found a stile
of upright stone, its opening too tight

for sheep, but wide enough for legs to file
one at a time between the tomb-like jambs,
thighs squeezing through the narrow slate-lined
    aisle.

Beyond were moorland walls in diagrams
descending to a lake, the only sounds
the hoot of owls, ewes calling to their lambs;

while down below, a house in modest grounds
looked out over the lake; and at its door
there stood a figure gazing at the bounds

of nature, covered in the moon's white hoar
who, when he saw us, cried out in a loud,
exalted Northern voice, 'See how before

us stretch the handiwork of hill and cloud,
which stimulate the philosophic mind
to deepest feeling. From my youth I vowed

to seek the simple pleasures of mankind
in rural isolation, and a wise
passiveness that leaves the world behind.

Welcome, you strangers, welcome to the prize
that nature offers to the purer soul –
the gift of seeing with our inward eyes

into the life of things, the glorious whole.'
Now ravenous with hunger, I replied,
'Sagacious poet, blessed be your goal

and ever may imagination glide
into your musings; yet I'd like to ask
if John and I might step a while inside

and rest our bones, and maybe fill our flask
from your good well. I'd like to hear you talk
at length about your vision and your task

once both of us recover from our walk
within the maze, where so far we have found
nothing but sterile twist and turn and baulk.

Perhaps through you we'll get to safer ground,
and you can tell us what's the best way out,
and if we're tackling it the right way round.'

The poet assented, 'Yes, without a doubt.
Tomorrow I will amplify my theme,
and intimate how you should go about

your quest, which is to find that blessed gleam
that never was on sea or land.' I stared,
then fell asleep. It all seemed like a dream.

When morning came, I found the Bard prepared
with volumes of his ballads open wide
at passages for which he greatly cared,

and which he read out with a proper pride.
'*In nature and the language of the sense,
the anchor of my purest thoughts*', he sighed,

'*the soul of all my moral being*', hence
'*a presence that disturbs me with the joy
of elevated thoughts,*' and (yet more tense),

'*Ye Presences of Nature in the sky
and on the earth! Ye Views of the hills
and Souls of lonely places!*' When a boy,

he'd seen '*the splendour in the grass which chills
with manhood, though the heart still feels
the motion and the spirit that impels*

all thinking things; the natural joy that heals.'
He paused as if in prayer, or else in praise.
He seemed a man who'd overcome ordeals,

and, thanking him, I asked if I might raise
my own concern of how I might escape,
beyond the stile, the clutches of the maze.

He said the alleys largely took the shape
of my imaginings, and I should look within.
'Reality,' he said, 'is but an ape

of the heart: unravel that, and you will win
release. Seek out the blessed mood where all
the burden of the mystery we're in –

this unintelligible world – grows small.
You'll find a heart that watches and receives
will serve you best when you re-cross the wall.'

But what, I thought, if the heart still deceives,
and setting suns lack the required effect?
Where can I then discover what relieves?

Where will I turn to find out what's correct?
As if he read my thoughts, he stared and cried,
'Trust Nature's works: we murder to dissect!

Describe things in themselves, unmodified
by any previous passion in your mind.
Allow the external object to provide

all necessary stimulus; leave behind
all preconceptions; let your feeling
reach out to the very simplest of mankind –

the beggar-man; the shepherd in his shieling.
Essential passions find a richer soil
in rustic life, where hearts are more revealing.

When simple souls throw off their mortal coil,
you'll find them rolled in earth's diurnal course,
their nature one which nothing more can spoil.'

He paused as if expecting we'd endorse
his utterance; and solemnly I said
he certainly had spoken with great force.

He gave us porridge and a crust of bread
to fortify us for our onward quest,
and so we once more took the way ahead,

wondering if we'd failed the Wordsworth test.

Canto Four

'From here,' John said, 'I find it hard to know
which routes lead on and which are cul-de-sacs.
Some are so muddy that you can't get through.

Others turn out to be such pygmy tracks,
you wish you'd never started. Here and there
you see a well-shaped opening – relax –

then find it's disappeared into thin air!
In one fine avenue a coach appears,
accompanied by dogs and dancing bear.

Its driver is a fan of Pope and steers
with great panache and devil-may-care, but fails
to stay the course and, changing horses, veers

between sharp satires and Satanic tales.
There is a wider highway we can take
which leads in turn to many other trails

and expeditions you may want to make,
but first a minor detour down this lane.'
We shortly reached a little house marked, 'Blake:

for *Songs* and *Heaven and Hell* and *Albion*,
enquire within.' 'I bring you here,' said John,
'to see a man who works against the grain

and will not let himself be put upon;
whose verse tells how society decays;
who won't rest till all dogma's dead and gone;

who tries to show us how to mend our ways
and wash away the cobwebs from the doors
of our perception, to reveal displays

of infinity in everything. He pours
out canticles of prophecy and dream,
claiming what dogmas damage, love restores.'

'Not bad,' I thought. 'Such a man might redeem
me from the maze. Perhaps a seer's eye
of intuition can produce a scheme

for imminent escape. It's worth a try.
I'll pull the bell and ask if he's a key
to open any exit door nearby.'

'You may discover,' said my guide, 'that he
produces maps you cannot understand,
and speaks of nothing but eternity.'

There now appeared a piercing eye which scanned
our face and garments. 'Strangers,' said a voice,
'I fear you're beached on life's unhappy strand,

like all who seek my wisdom and advice.
Be certain that this world is counterfeit.
Imagination is your only choice

if you would live. Nature is pure deceit.
Desire and act, and you will find delight.
Only through vision can we be complete.'

These Delphic words did not shed instant light
on my predicament, and I replied,
'Good Sir, indeed I seek help with my plight,

but your prescription leaves me mystified.
Imagination can elicit fear,
and some desires are best not gratified.

Dreams which seem solid quickly disappear
and the cold light of day brings disillusion.
And how can we distinguish well and clear

the true Jerusalem from a delusion?
Can vision shorn of reason ever hope
to save us from our follies and confusion?

Is it not intellect which gives us scope
to build Jerusalems on solid ground –
Newtonian structures which can help us cope?'

At this, the Lambeth visionary frowned
and shook his head. 'You'd better come inside,'
he said, 'and see the evidence around.

My prints and my prophetic books provide
the vision that you lack, and will reveal
the inner light which is our only guide.'

An hour or two and I began to feel
a second maze was growing in my head:
his genius was not a power to heal,

but an apocalypse where living dead
moved through a grim Miltonic congeries
of myth piled upon myth, with no light shed

on daily, less dramatic mysteries.
'Cathartic, maybe, when the show is done,'
I thought, 'but at this point the vista is

unpromising. No answers here. Move on.'
And so we left the seer with his Books
of Los, Ahania and Urizen.

We couldn't help but notice filthy looks,
although we'd praised his love of liberty
and tenderness to children. 'O for brooks,'

said John, 'and nightingales, and melody.
Back to the wider road of which I spoke,
to find a bard who's not so finicky.'

As evening fell, we saw a curl of smoke
above a sort of chemist's shop, with jars
of coloured liquids; curtains like a cloak

of gold; blue Delft-ware pots; a Grecian vase.
The tableau was well set, but where was Keats?
Outside, a figure moved beneath the stars.

'I have been dreaming up some new conceits,'
he said, 'and watched you swim into my ken
like tired oarsmen weary on their seats,

your clothes as foul as a bedraggled hen.
What have you lost? And why so woebegone
and palely loitering beside my den?'

Our story told, 'No wonder you're so wan,
after the pantheist of Ambleside,'
he smiled, 'and by the Tyger put upon.

There is no magic way to help you glide
past all these strange conjunctions. Only joy
and beauty have the power to be your guide,

and suffering. I don't wish to destroy
your hopes but each must find his own way out
of entanglement. The best way's to deploy

the inner music we can't do without
into a well-turned verse, and make a song.
Then watch those sharp thorns wither all about!'

'Escape through Poesy?' I thought. 'But not for long!
He said himself that *fancy cannot cheat
so well as fam'd*. He's surely got it wrong?'

And asked, 'But don't all poets face defeat?
What of unfinished *Kubla, Christabel*?
Isn't the end more often sour than sweet?'

'We do what we can,' he answered, 'to rebel
against the inarticulate. If we succeed,
and in what measure, only time will tell.

I follow in the path where others lead.
Chaucer and Shakespeare, Spenser, Milton show
how peerless words can penetrate

and bleed into the heart. That's how we grow.'
We listened to him well into the night,
until the march of mind began to slow,

and, in the East, we saw the morning light.

Canto Five

By now my guide was anxious to return
to his neglected garden; we agreed
to part. 'You have begun,' he said, 'to learn

how to unthread the labyrinth; you don't need
my ministrations any more; the worst
is over. Though the maze will still mislead –

directions which seem clear will be reversed –
all you will ever lose is sleep and sweat.'
He pointed westwards. 'That's the way, but first

you'll find the going heavy, stale and wet –
downstream from Keats there is a kind of slough.
Don't linger there. Press on without regret

to drier country and a higher brow.'
With that he shook my hand and said goodbye,
leaving me silent, wondering – 'what now?'

For days I wandered under a fitful sky
past dreadful hollows, little woods and lakes
where knights in armour and their dames passed by,

pied pipers, people bringing news from Aix,
forsaken mermen, fairies, *fleurs du mal*,
funereal elegies of various makes;

a pageant so diverse it needed sal
volatile, so full of artifice
it left me gasping for fresh air. 'How shall

I manage to escape,' I mused, 'from this
kaleidoscope of *weltschmerz* and decay,
this mix of rich brocades and restlessness?'

But on I struggled, taking every day
the driest path, and seeking higher ground.
Far to the North a parsonage caught my eye,

but I could see no route beyond its mound.
To the South, a voiceless ghost; and to the West,
the twilight. Where now? 'Hi, my name is Pound,'

I heard behind me, 'Why not take a rest
and tell me who you are and what you do?
If you've got time, I'll show you where the best

roads are, and where to get the finest view.
My task here is to attack the undergrowth
and turn the landscape into something new.'

'A hacker down of hedges? Then we're both
in the same business,' I replied. 'My way
is yours; just show me how. I am no sloth

when it comes to slash and burn.' Then Ezra: 'Say!
I like your style, but could you tell me why
you're writing terza rima in this day

and age? Dante is fine, but get your eye
on something later, like the *Leaves of Grass*.
Forget the Vallombrosa. Time goes by.

You ought to come and hear my masterclass
with Yeats and Eliot. Possum's too abstruse,
and Willie over-writes – there's too much gas

and colouring. I've warned him to abuse
less adjectives and take some dead nouns out.
Abstractions in my canon are obtuse:

my manifesto leaves no room for doubt
that iambs fetter; cadence must take their place.
Without me, Eliot was up the spout

with *The Waste Land*; and though he had the grace
to call me *miglior fabbro* when we'd done,
how else could he have looked me in the face?'

He sounded like a man who knew he'd won,
and was determined not to undersell;
but when I asked how his own work had gone,

'I started off,' he said, 'with Provençal,
and went on to Li Po and other ware
from China; then Propertius and a trawl

around my own *musée imaginaire*.
But what I put together was a botch:
a toss of dice suspended in mid-air:

a diffidence that faltered. Lost my touch.'
'A moment of humility,' I thought,
'is worth an age of brag, however much

it costs, even if it means you're under-bought.
He lopped the hedge, but landed in the ditch –
it's not a lesson I'd want to be taught.'

'What in the end,' I asked him, 'gave you the itch
to write? What made you put your acumen
into prosody? Why not paint or stitch?'

'It's what I'm made for,' he said. 'I take my pen
while others take a brush. The ideogram,
the image, song, are all my life's dimension.

Poetry's the real thing - makes me what I am.
My poems are the patterns that I see.
As for the end, I couldn't give a damn,

unlike the Possum with his theology,
or Yeats, who told the horseman to pass by,
but really longed for immortality.

I am a kind of teacher; put my eye
and ear at the service of the few
who care to look and listen while I try

to erect antennae, catch what is new,
and, for my age and time, communicate.'
I took this final dictum as my cue

to ask which path to take. 'There is no gate,'
he said, 'through which you can escape the maze.
The way to manage is to gravitate

towards the clearest view on offer, ways
that seem to show a hint of what comes next;
then build yourself a refuge for the days

of isolation, when you're sick or vexed;
a place where you can hold things in suspense
and turn your perturbation into text,

construing till refractory words make sense,
and stubborn phrases constitute a theme;
a place of quarantine and convalescence where

you rise robust from an austere regime;
a place where you can keep the inward eye
focussed on vision, image, omen, dream.'

'This,' I thought, 'is the line I'll have to buy.
I'll find a refuge, but not too remote,
and build myself a tower, but not too high

or full of bibelots, as an antidote
to the labyrinth; where I can retreat
like Yeats or Ruskin to a niche, and note

time's passage in a capsule, bitter-sweet.'
And yet there was a point which Pound had missed
in his prescription. Was rhyme obsolete?

'You asked me why I bothered to persist
with terza rima. It's the power,' I said,
'of a well-tuned engine. No ventriloquist

free verse has got the throttle or the cred.
Cadence is subtle, but can be illusory
and roll into the sand. Rhyme stays in the head,

and stacks; avoids just-what-you-choosery.'
The poet shook his head and went off fast,
muttering darkly about graft and usury,

abuse of Dante, and my dubious past
and unpropitious future. I resigned
myself to stoical endurance. 'Blast

the maze, but I must take it as I find
it, and make do!' I cried, as I set out
to stake my ground where I was most inclined,

and build my wall, my tower, my redoubt.